THE VALUE OF A *Woman*

God's Blueprint for
Discovering Identity, Developing Excellence,
and Fulfilling Purpose

Dr. Veronica Deas

THE VALUE OF A WOMAN

Published by Publish Your Gift®
An imprint of Purposely Created Publishing Group, LLC

Scripture quotations are taken from the Holy Bible, unless otherwise noted.

Printed in the United States of America

ISBN: 978-1-64484-675-9 (print)
ISBN: 978-1-64484-675-9 (ebook)

THE
VALUE
Woman
OF A

TABLE OF CONTENTS

INTRODUCTION

In 2013, the Holy Spirit spoke to me about a woman's value—a revelation that would transform how I understood the divine design and purpose of women in God's kingdom and on this earth.

While everyone possesses inherent value, I want to specifically emphasize why a woman is so uniquely valuable and what this means for her.

Let's talk about value. Value has three parts: how important something is, how much something is worth, and how useful something is. In this book, we will look at: The Importance of a Woman, The Worth of a Woman, and The Assignment (Usefulness) of a Woman.

A woman is important because of her significance, her God-given abilities, and her divine purpose. Purpose is the reason something is created. A woman was created to be helpful, extraordinary, and worthy of attention. She was designed by God with importance, worth, and usefulness for the earth.

A woman commands attention because she possesses the ability to change the atmosphere. She can change it for good or bad, depending on her knowledge or ignorance of her value as a woman. When she understands her true value, she recognizes her qualities and abilities and comprehends why God placed her on this earth.

There is a Scripture that captures God's heart for our purpose and prosperity: "Beloved, I wish above all things that thou mayest prosper and be in health, even as thy soul prospers" (3 John 2). The goal is to prosper in everything in life—your spirit, body, mind, will, and emotions.

For true prosperity to occur, identity must be established. You must know who you are, where you came from, and where you are going. Let's begin this journey of discovering a woman's true value.

CHAPTER 1

THE IMPORTANCE OF A WOMAN

Every woman should know her value and purpose. A woman's value shows up in three ways: her importance, her worth, and how useful she is in God's plan for her life.

Society's False Narrative

The term "woman" has been misused in today's society. Society tells women they should "know their place"—stay in the kitchen and bedroom. Sadly, some women have believed these lies and have stopped growing in their God-given purpose.

The Divine Definition

The Hebrew word for woman is "isha." It comes from Eve being taken from man's side. The book of Genesis says: "This is now bone of my bones, and flesh of my flesh: she shall be called Woman, because she was taken out of Man." The word "isha" means to protect and to rule.

A woman was design to protect and rule the environment with a man.

Apostle Isi Igenegba said, "A female is a gender, but a woman is a spiritual office given by God Himself."

In the late Dr. Myles Munroe's books, *The Power and Purpose of Women* and *The Power and Purpose of Men,* he emphasized that man has authoritative power and woman has influential power.

According to the dictionary, influential power is the ability to change or affect others' behavior, thoughts, or attitudes, not through force, but through persuasion, relationships, and trust.

Through influence, woman has the power to shift the entire earth. *See Genesis 3:1-7.*

God's Original Design

The original plan for woman is to exist in God's image and likeness, to rule and reign alongside man on Earth. Genesis 1:26-27 tells us: "God said, 'Let us make man in Our image, after Our likeness: and let them have dominion over the fish of the sea, and over the fowl of the air, and over the cattle, and over all the earth, and over every creeping thing that creepeth upon the earth.' So God created man in His own image, in the image of God created He him; male and female created He them."

A woman possesses great value because she represents God on Earth. When God declared, "It is not good that man should be alone; I will make a help meet for him," He was establishing woman's vital role. God designed her as a helper to assist man with divine tasks. Both male and female were created within man, and when God formed woman from man's rib, He gave both dominion to rule and reign on Earth. In the natural, a rib protects the heart and the lungs. The heart represents life and the lungs represent breath. A woman has the ability to help while protecting life.

Divine Partnership and Completeness

God made man and woman to partner together with dominion and destiny to inhabit the Earth. A woman is important because she completes man, just as man completes woman. She was taken from man, meaning his completeness exists within woman, and her completeness exists within man. They need each other to fulfill their destiny and purpose on Earth.

In God's design, man and woman operate as a team, the man gives and the woman receives. A woman has the amazing ability to conceive man's seed, carry the seed until the baby is formed for birth, and then raise and care for new life. What she knows about the importance of her value will decide if she helps life grow or lets death win.

Without woman, there would be no birthing on Earth. Without birth, the earth would eventually become depleted and desolate.

The Divine Enhancer

Woman was made to make things better. She can strengthen and improve everything she touches. Her role is to nurture her surroundings by growing and developing those around her. She develops in wisdom, which produces knowledge and good judgement. She is able to guide with strength, gentleness, and diligence.

It is crucial that every woman understands her value, recognizes why God placed her on Earth, and comprehends how her value can change destiny.

Environmental Influence

A woman can influence her environment.

Environment means everything around us that affects our lives, growth, health, and how we do things. So, a woman can multiply what's around her. She can influence it toward growth or toward stagnation.

Because of her influential power, she is able to multiply her circumstances, conditions, and influences, affecting everyone she encounters. She has the ability to strengthen and improve everything she touches. Man needs woman to strengthen and improve his quality of life. The saying "behind every successful man is a successful woman" reflects the original divine design—each needs the other for completion and success.

Biblical Examples of Enhancement or Influence

Consider Abigail in 1 Samuel 25. This wise woman used her abilities and influence to save King David's destiny. Though married to Nabal, a foolish man who disrespected David and his men, Abigail intervened when David planned to destroy all the men in their land. Filled with wisdom, she used her enhancement skills to spare her household and preserve David's destiny as future king. David was so impressed with Abigail that after her husband's death, he married her.

Deborah served as prophetess, leader, and judge in Israel (Judges 4-5). She strengthened and improved the people through her ability to hear from God and provide wise judgment. When God revealed that Israel would win an upcoming battle, she encouraged the army captain to go and conquer. However, he refused to enter battle unless she accompanied him—he needed her presence for confidence. They won the battle, but God gave the final honor to another woman, Jael, who softly killed the enemy captain.

Each woman was acknowledged and honored because of her ability to strengthen and improve her environment.

Modern Understanding of Woman's Purpose

The late Dr. Myles Munroe, a powerful spiritual leader, wrote extensively about the purpose of women. In *Understanding the Purpose and Power of Women*, he identified several unique qualities that emphasize the significance women bring to Earth. According to Dr. Munroe, a woman is an enhancer, a reflector, and a life-giver.

As an enhancer, whatever you give a woman, she will strengthen and improve. Give her honor, and she will multiply honor. Give her dishonor, and she will multiply dishonor.

As a reflector, she mirrors what you give her. We must be careful about our behavior around the women in our lives, as they will eventually reflect what we give them.

As a life-giver, woman not only births humans; woman can also birth vision. If a man lacks vision, division will be born instead. Women were created to be productive, not passive. Without vision from the man, she will produce her own vision.

This is why it's important for men to have vision for women to help bring to pass.

The Proverbs 31 Standard

The Proverbs 31 woman represents the importance of womanhood at its finest. She is a woman of devotion who fears and loves God. Her price is above rubies, meaning she demands and expects respect and honor. She is an entrepreneur and investor who supports her husband and excels as a mother. She operates in wisdom, and her husband calls her blessed.

Every woman should understand her importance in order to fulfill her fullest potential and walk in the excellence God designed for her life.

Key Spiritual Lessons

The *Importance of a Woman* teaches us:

1. A woman is not merely a gender distinction, but a spiritual office established by God with influence, authority, and purpose.
2. Woman was created to protect, enhance, and rule the environment, partnering with man to fulfill God's dominion mandate.
3. A woman's influence has the power to multiply life or stagnation, depending on her understanding of her value.
4. When a woman understands her importance, she becomes an atmosphere changer, strengthening and improving everything she touches.

Biblical Foundations

Key Scriptures that anchor these lessons are:

- **Genesis 1:26–27** – God created male and female in His image and gave them dominion over the earth.
- **Genesis 2:18** – God declared that it was not good for man to be alone and created woman as a divinely appointed helper.
- **Proverbs 31:10** – A virtuous woman's value is far above rubies, reflecting her importance and worth.
- **1 Samuel 25** – Abigail's wisdom and influence preserved David's destiny and transformed her environment.

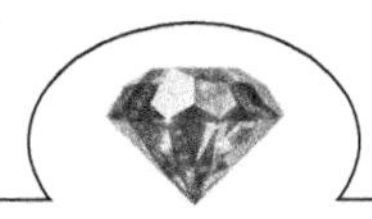

Reflect and Activate
Identity and Divine Importance

How has society's definition of womanhood shaped the way you view your importance, and where does that definition conflict with God's original design?

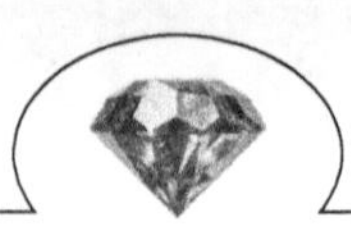

In what environments (home, work, ministry, relationships) has God positioned you to protect, enhance, or rule, but you may have underestimated your influence?

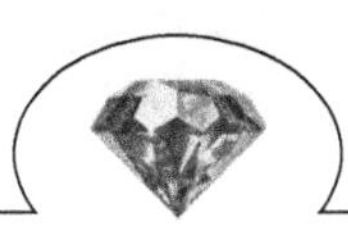

Abigail and Deborah used wisdom to change outcomes. Where is God calling you to use your influence to preserve life, peace, or destiny?

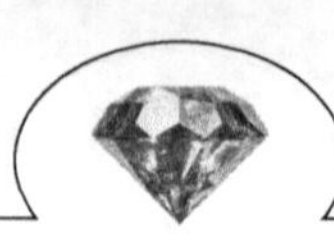

What practical step can you take this week to activate your importance and intentionally improve the atmosphere around you?

C H A P T E R 2

THE WORTH OF A WOMAN

We've talked about how important women are in God's plan. Now let's look at a woman's worth. Remember, value has three parts: importance, worth, and usefulness.

Worth means how valuable you are. A woman shows her worth through her abilities—her skills and talents. The more she develops these abilities, the more excellent she becomes.

Developing Abilities and Excellence

Hidden within every woman are treasures designed to create and enhance her environment. A woman has the ability to build her worth by investing in herself, increasing her skills and talents, and developing a character of excellence. She must be outstanding in everything she does.

A woman should always engage in purposeful activity. She should be able to receive a vision and bring it to fruition. God designed her to make her world better. As she grows, her world grows too.

The Role of Cultivation

One important role of a man is to cultivate a woman—to make her better, not bitter. Instead of degrading a woman, a man should enhance her potential, giving her room to soar and become everything she was created to be.

As I said in the previous chapter, a man must maintain vision. If he doesn't, the woman will create her own vision, which may cause division in the home. He should create opportunities for her assistance and partnership.

Atmospheric Change and Dominion

Woman was made to change the atmosphere around her. Remember, God gave her the right to rule and reign with man. Where she lives and works will show her worth on Earth. She should be able to add to and multiply what's around her.

Essential Qualities of Worth

Quality means how good something is compared to other things like it. So, what qualities make a woman valuable?

> **Quality #1 - Helper and Completer:** She was designed to help complete divine tasks. Created in the image and likeness of God, she possesses God's power and creativity. She can create her environment and help man rule the earth.

- **Quality #2 - Assistant and Supporter:** She was made to assist and support in accomplishing God's purposes on Earth. She engages in the development of others.

- **Quality #3 - Receiver:** She possesses the divine capacity to receive what is given to her.

- **Quality #4 - Incubator and Developer:** She can grow what she receives, taking care of it and helping it develop until it's time to give birth and multiply the results.

- **Quality #5 - Adaptor:** She can connect effectively to her environment. However, a woman must be careful about her environment because it will influence her development and output.

- **Quality #6 - Reflector:** She reflects what she receives, making it crucial that she receives positive, life-giving input.

The Blue Diamond Principle

The Holy Spirit gave me the symbol of the blue diamond to represent a woman's value. A real blue diamond is one of the rarest gems in the world. One carat is worth over a million dollars and can only be found in three places: Australia, South Africa, and India. Many people want a blue diamond, but only a few can afford something so precious. Similarly, a woman is rare and exquisite. Her value is priceless. She should be admired and recognized as extraordinary. A man must be willing to pay a high price to obtain a woman of worth. The more she lives out her true purpose, the more valuable she becomes.

Increasing Your Worth

A woman must increase her value by developing her worth. She must enhance her qualities and abilities, becoming a woman of excellence. She must grow in discernment—the ability to judge well. As she increases in her qualities, her worth increases, and she becomes priceless like the blue diamond. She must become so valuable that she influences others to become their best.

The Completion Principle

A woman's worth is significant because she came from man's rib—she completes him. For both to be whole, they need connection with each other to fulfill their divine purpose. This partnership is essential for both to thrive. Without woman, mankind would become extinct. She is vital to the existence and continuation of humanity.

Using a house as an analogy: if man is the foundation, woman is the frame and decoration. If the foundation is unstable, the entire house becomes dysfunctional. When a man doesn't function in his designed purpose, the woman will begin functioning in his capacity to maintain stability.

Your Priceless Value

Women, don't allow others to devalue you by preventing your growth and development. Increasing your skills and abilities will make you invaluable to your environment and purpose.

You are valuable—make your mark and become that authentic blue diamond. Arise and shine; it's time to live in the fullness of your worth!

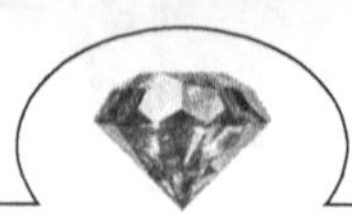

Key Spiritual Lessons

The *Worth of a Woman* teaches us:

1. A woman's worth is revealed through the development of her abilities, not merely through potential or intention.
2. God designed women to increase in value as they grow in excellence, wisdom, and discernment.
3. Cultivation—both self-cultivation and wise partnership—plays a critical role in whether a woman becomes bitter or better.
4. When a woman commits to excellence, her worth becomes priceless, influencing others and elevating her environment.

Biblical Foundations

Key Scriptures that anchor these lessons are:

- **Proverbs 18:16** – A person's gift makes room for them and brings them before great people.
- **Proverbs 22:29** – Those who excel in their work will stand before kings and not before mere men.
- **Ecclesiastes 10:10** – Wisdom brings advantage and success, emphasizing the value of skill development.
- **Genesis 2:21–22** – Woman was formed from man's rib, signifying her role as a completer and partner in purpose.

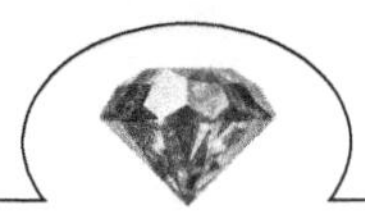

Reflect and Activate

Excellence and Worth

What abilities or skills has God placed within you that require further development to reflect excellence?

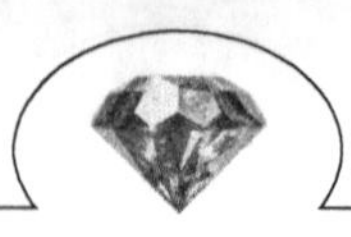

In what areas of your life have you settled for potential instead of committing to growth and refinement?

How has your environment influenced your sense of worth—for better or for worse—and what adjustments are needed?

What intentional action can you take to increase your value by investing in your gifts, character, or wisdom?

CHAPTER 3

THE ASSIGNMENT OF A WOMAN

We have explored the importance and worth of women. Now, let's examine the final element of value: assignment (usefulness).

Usefulness means being helpful and having beneficial relevance. Usefulness also shows how excellent something is for the task given.

Once a woman identifies her importance and worth, she is able to be usefulness in every situation. She stirs up the abilities and gifts that are within her. She begins to create with her words and shift her world to produce life.

According to Proverbs 18:21, "Death and life are in the power of the tongue, and they that love it shall eat the fruit thereof."

She recognizes she was created to rule and reign with man. She is a helper. She has qualities to improve her environment. She is an enhancer, developer, and a powerful influencer. She can change her environment through her abilities and her level of excellence.

The Chess Queen Principle

Think about the game of chess. On the chessboard, the queen is the most powerful piece. When she gets close to the action, she can move in many directions, making her dangerous to the other side. The queen can protect the king and, as the most powerful piece, serves as the most effective defender. But because she's so valuable, enemies will target her.

God is the master chess player with checkmate power. He uses women—those considered the "weaker vessel"— to triumph in life's battles. He makes women useful to populate the land and empower men.

A woman of value knows her identity and can protect her environment. She makes herself useful by increasing her skills and abilities, walking in excellence, and making her life profitable and beneficial. She uses wisdom to guide her environment.

Hidden Figures: Excellence in Action

The movie *Hidden Figures* shows how women can grow their skills and abilities to help with extraordinary achievements. In this case, they helped astronauts go to the moon.

The astronauts got the praise as the first men in space during the 1960s Mercury missions. But behind the scenes, hundreds of unrecognized NASA workers supported them. This included "human computers" who calculated flight paths.

Three of these workers are recognize as brilliant African-American women—Katherine Johnson, Dorothy Vaughan, and Mary Jackson—who were behind the scenes, sending astronaut John Glenn into space. This amazing success gave the nation confidence, helped America win the Space Race, and inspired the world.

The astronauts were the visible heroes, but the mathematical precision of these women provided the essential foundation for success.

These women showed usefulness through their excellence and abilities, leveraging numbers to accomplish extraordinary realities.

Maximizing Your Assignment

A woman maximizes her assignment by:

1. Developing her skills and abilities to the highest level of excellence.

2. Understanding her environment and how to positively influence it.

3. Embracing her role as an enhancer in every situation she encounters.

4. Using wisdom to guide decisions and relationships.

5. Recognizing her strategic value in God's plan.

6. Refusing to minimize her contributions or hide her capabilities.

7. Stepping into opportunities to demonstrate her unique gifts.

Fulfilling Your Purpose

Every woman has a divine assignment that requires her unique combination of importance, worth, and usefulness. When you understand and embrace all three elements of your value, you become unstoppable in fulfilling your purpose.

You are not an accident or an afterthought in God's design. You are a strategic, valuable, and useful part of His plan for Earth. Your importance establishes your identity, your worth determines your impact, and your usefulness fulfills your purpose.

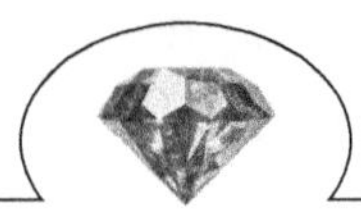

Key Spiritual Lessons

The *Usefulness of a Woman* teaches us:

1. A woman becomes most useful when she understands her identity and worth and applies them with wisdom and excellence.
2. God designed women to be strategic contributors, not passive participants, in fulfilling divine assignments.
3. A woman's usefulness is activated through her words, skills, and discernment, which shape outcomes and environments.
4. When a woman fully embraces her usefulness, she becomes a powerful force for protection, productivity, and purpose.

Biblical Foundations

Key Scriptures that anchor these lessons are:

- **Proverbs 18:21** – Death and life are in the power of the tongue; words activate outcomes.
- **Ecclesiastes 9:10** – Whatever your hand finds to do, do it with all your might.
- **Judges 4–5** – Deborah's leadership demonstrates usefulness through wisdom, courage, and obedience to God.
- **1 Corinthians 12:18** – God places each part in the body exactly where He wants it, affirming strategic usefulness.

Reflect and Activate
Assignment and Execution

Where is God currently calling you to apply your abilities, not just acknowledge them?

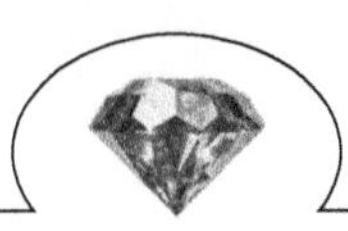

In what areas have you minimized your usefulness due to fear, comparison, or lack of confidence?

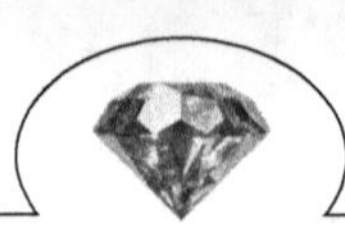

How are your words shaping your environment—are they producing life, direction, and clarity?

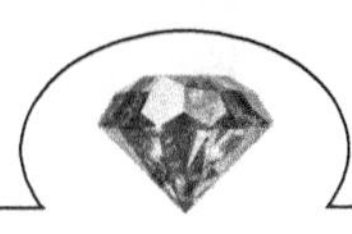

What specific step can you take now to operate boldly in your divine assignment?

CONCLUSION

A woman's value has three parts: her importance, worth, and assignment (usefulness) in God's plan. She was created in God's image, given the right to rule, and made to be an important partner in doing God's work on Earth.

As an enhancer, reflector, and life-giver, woman possesses unique qualities that make her invaluable to God's plan. Like the rare blue diamond, her authentic value increases as she walks in her divine purpose.

Through biblical examples like Abigail and Deborah, and modern examples like the mathematicians in *Hidden Figures*, we see how women change atmospheres, save destinies, and provide the essential foundation for extraordinary achievements.

Every woman must recognize her importance, develop her worth, and maximize her assignment. When she does, she becomes the woman God created her to be—powerful, purposeful, and priceless.

The revelation the Holy Spirit gave me in 2013 remains true today: women are valuable beyond measure, designed for greatness, and essential to God's purposes on Earth.

It's time for every woman to arise, shine, and live in the fullness of her God-given value!

The world needs what God has placed within you. Your importance, worth, and assignment are not optional—they are essential to the divine plan.

Step into your value. Embrace your purpose. Transform your world!

ABOUT THE AUTHOR

Dr. Veronica Deas is a passionate educator, author, speaker, and faith leader whose life mission is simple yet profound: *"Know who you are and Whose you are."* With over 30 years of teaching experience, she has inspired thousands through her work in education, as well as her leadership with the *Value of a Woman* organization, where she spearheads conferences and hosts a dynamic podcast.

Dr. Deas holds a B.A. in Accounting, an MBA, and an Ed.D. in Educational and Organizational Leadership—credentials that reflect both her intellectual rigor and her commitment to equipping others for growth. Blending her love for studying God's Word, teaching, fashion, and storytelling, she brings a unique voice to the intersection of faith and practical living.

A resident of Goose Creek, South Carolina, Dr. Deas now turns her decades of wisdom toward empowering readers through her literary publications.

www.ingramcontent.com/pod-product-compliance
Lightning Source LLC
Chambersburg PA
CBHW061441050726
47593CB00004B/1412